I0428848

Couch Critic
Catalog

Cari Lynn Vaughn

© Copyright 2016 Cari Lynn Vaughn

Purple Rose Ink Publications

ISBN-13: 978-1532777578
ISBN-10: 1532777574

Introduction

Most of the movies I watched as a child were on TV and on video. I am sure I watched quite a lot, as most people my age were inclined to do. As a teenager, I did write down movies I saw at the theater on a calendar and sometimes mentioned them in my diary entries. However, I didn't get the idea to start keeping track of what I was watching in list form until my late 20s.

In the year 2000, I took to my local Blockbuster and wandered the aisles with a pen and paper. I wrote down all movies I'd remembered seeing. Then I went home and added to my list by looking over old calendars and diaries. I also consulted Leonard Martin's 2000 movie guide. Between all of those sources, I was able to compile a pretty comprehensive list.

In the years to come, I started writing down movies I viewed shortly after I viewed them. Despite being pretty busy, I was able to watch a great many movies each year. With the advent of DVDs and Netflix, I was able to binge watch entire seasons of shows I didn't get to watch on TV or seasons I caught part of enough, but not in their entirety.

I am not sure if I watch more than the average viewer, but I think that I probably have. I read that the average person in 2015 only goes to about 5 movies year at the theater, but tends to watch 20-30 per year on video, which seems about right. In any case, if I watched 35 movies a year and I've been watching movies for 35 years, I will have watched over 1,200 movies. I haven't added up all the movies and shows from this list, but I am sure it is well over that

I went to the theater every couple of weeks for a while in the 90s, but once I had kids, going to the movies becomes a huge expensive event, so it doesn't happen often any more. Watching movies at home is cheaper and easier and with streaming, kids can watch what they want and you can watch you want as an adult.

So here is my back list of movies from 1980 to 2000—twenty years essentially. And though I was born in 1976, I have enjoyed many older movies over the years. I often heard movies like *Casablanca* and the *Maltese Falcon* referenced in other movies and TV shows, so I had to watch them. I watched a lot of TV as a kid and I still do, so I listed TV shows I watched and DVDs of TV shows I watched as well.

There are a few pages at the end that list the VHS tapes and DVDs I own. I began replacing VHS with DVDs slowly through the 2000s. Finally, in 2015, I got rid of all my VHS.

Movies

(Backlog Movie List)

*Boring **Entertaining Enough***Good ****Awesome

Nosforatu		**	Class
Wuthering Heights	1939	***	TV
Camille		**	Video
The Mummy		***	TV
Dracula (1931)		**	TV
The Canterville Ghost		**	Video
A Tale Of Two Cities		**	Class
Great Expectations		**	Class
It's A Wonderful Life		*****	TV
To Kill A Mockingbird		****	TV
A Little Princess		***	TV
Heidi		***	TV
The Little Colonel		**	TV
Poor Little Rich Girl		**	TV
Casablanca		****	TV
Maltese Falcon		***	Video
Key Largo		***	TV
The Valley of the Kings		***	TV
Payton Place		**	Video
Long Hot Summer		***	Video

African Queen	***	Video
The Time Machine	***	TV
The Fly	**	TV
With Six You Get Egg Roll	**	TV
Please Don't Eat The Daisies	**	TV
The Apartment	****	Video
Sweet Charity	***	Video
On A Clear Day You Can See Forever	***	TV
An Affair To Remember	****	Video
Breakfast At Tiffany's	***	Video
Wait Until Dark	***	Video
National Velvet	***	Re-Release
The Taming Of The Shrew	***	Class
Henry V	**	Class
Midsummer Night's Dream	**	Class
Camelot	*	Video
South Pacific	*	Class
The Wizard Of OZ	****	TV
The Sound Of Music	****	TV
My Fair Lady	***	TV
Love Story	***	TV
West Side Story	***	TV
Grease	***	TV

The Way We Were	***	TV
Romeo And Juliet 1968	****	TV
The Smurfs And The Magic Flute	***	TV
Snow White And The Seven Dwarfs	***	TV
Sleeping Beauty	***	TV
Bambi	***	TV
Pinococio	**	TV
Peter Pan	**	TV
The Sword And The Stone	***	TV
Dumbo	**	TV
Cinderella	***	TV
The Lady And The Tramp	****	TV
101 Dalmatians	***	TV
Alice In Wonderland	***	TV
Pollyanna	***	TV
The Parent Trap	***	TV
The Trouble With Angels	**	TV
That Darn Cat	***	TV
Gidget	**	TV
Mary Poppins	***	TV
Chitty-Chitty Bang Bang	**	TV
Bedknobs And Broomsticks	**	TV
The Incredible Mr. Limpit	**	TV

The Absent Minded Professor	**	TV
The Hound Of The Baskervilles	***	Class
The Fall Of The House Of Usher	**	Class
The Innocents	***	Class
Rebecca	***	Class
Death In Venice	**	Class
My Father's Triumph (French)	***	Class
Pocket Change (French)	**	Class
The Rose	****	TV
Inherit The Wind	***	TV
Charlotte's Web	***	Class
The Hobbit	****	Class
The Lord Of The Rings	***	TV
The Clash Of The Titans	**	TV
Puff The Magic Dragon	**	TV
Escape To Witch Mountain	***	TV
Return To Witch Mountain	***	TV
Clockwork Orange	***	Video
Up in Smoke	**	Video
Monty Python's Meaning Of Life	***	Video
The Jerk	**	TV
Freaky Friday	**	TV
American Graffiti	***	TV

80's Movies

Star Wars 1977	****	Theater Re-release
Empire Strikes Back	****	Theater Re-release
Return Of The Jedi	****	Theater Re-release
ET: The Extra Terrestrial	****	Theater
Popeye	***	Drive In
The Muppet Movie	**	TV
The Muppet's Take Manhattan	**	TV
Annie	***	Video
A Christmas Story	***	TV
The Last Unicorn	****	TV
The Princess Bride	****	Video
Lady Hawk	****	Video
Labyrinth	****	Video
Legend	***	Video
Goonies	****	Video
Gremlins	**	Video
Trolls	**	TV
Spaceballs	***	Video
The Last Star Fighter	***	Video
Starman	***	Video
Star Trek: The Voyage Home	***	Video
Star Trek: The Final Frontier	**	Video

Not Quite Human	**	Video
Howard The Duck	**	Video
D.A.R.Y.L.	***	Video
Flight Of The Navigator	***	Video
The Time Bandits	***	Video
Something Wicked This Way Comes	**	Video
Somewhere In Time	***	Video
Fame	***	Video
Space Camp	****	Video
Adventures In Babysitting	***	Video
American Anthem	***	Video
The Canterville Ghost	****	Video
Officer And A Gentleman	***	Video
Heaven Can Wait	**	Video
Journey Of Natty Gan	***	Video
The Color Purple	***	Video
Clara's Heart	***	Video
The Turning Point	****	Video
Terms Of Endearment	****	TV
Out On A Limb	****	TV
Cocoon	**	Video
Beastmaster	***	Video
Masters of the Universe	*	Video

Conan the Barbarian	*	Video
Baby	***	Video
Batteries Not Included	**	Video
Short Circuit	**	Video
Short Circuit 2	**	Video
Weird Science	**	Video
Spies Like Us	**	Video
Top Secret	**	Video
Ferris Bueller's Day Off	***	Video
Harry And The Henderson's	***	Video
Mystic Pizza	***	Video
Sixteen Candles	***	TV
Breakfast Club	****	TV
Pretty In Pink	***	TV
Satisfaction	***	TV
Black Widow	**	Video
Superman	***	TV
Superman 2	**	TV
Superman 3	**	TV
Superman 4	*	TV
The Karate Kid	***	Video
The Karate Kid 2	***	Video
Ghostbusters	**	Drive In

Ghostbusters 2	**	Video
Airplane	**	TV
Airplane 2	**	TV
Police Academy Movies	*	TV
Lampoon's Family Vacation	***	TV
Lampoon's European Vacation	**	TV
Money Pit	**	TV
Hello Again	***	Video
Outrageous Fortune	***	Video
Ruthless People	**	Video
Down And Out In Beverly Hills	**	TV
Camp Beverly Hills	**	TV
Two Moon Junction	*	Video
9 1/2 Weeks	***	Video
Risky Business	***	Video
The Color Of Money	***	Video
Top Gun	***	Video
All The Right Moves	***	TV
Stand By Me	***	Video
The Blue Lagoon	***	Video
Return To OZ	**	Video
The Peanut Butter Solution	*	TV
The Boy Who Could Fly	***	TV

Neverending Story	**	Video
Anne Of Green Gables	****	TV
A Friendship In Vienna	****	TV
A Passage To India	***	Class
Romancing The Stone	***	Video
Jewel Of The Nile	**	Video
War Of The Roses	**	Video
Heathers	***	Video
Overboard	***	Video
Working Woman	***	Video
Working 9-5	***	TV
Gorillas In The Mist	***	Video
Shag	***	Video
Desperately Seeking Susan	**	TV
Beatlejuice	***	Video
Edward Scissorhands	***	Video
Cat People	**	TV
Secret Of My Success	**	TV
Back To The Future	***	Theater
Tootsie	**	TV
Nadia	***	TV
Crocodile Dundee	**	Video
Summer Rental	**	TV

Great Outdoors	**	TV
Uncle Buck	**	TV
Summer School	***	TV
Little Monsters	**	Video
Amadeus	***	Video
The Three Amigos	**	Video
The Naked Gun	**	Video
Inner Space	**	TV
Moonstruck	**	Video
Witches Of Eastwick	**	Video
Raiders of the Lost Ark	****	Video
Temple of Doom	***	Video
Last Crusade	****	Theater
Honey I Shrunk The Kids	**	Theater
Young Sherlock Holmes	***	Video
Fatal Attraction	***	Video
The Accused	***	Video
Reversal Of Fortune	***	TV
Kenneth Brannigan's Henry V	***	Video
Gleaming The Cube	***	TV
Who's That Girl	*	TV
She's Out Of Control	**	Video
The Three Fugitives	*	Video

Little Shop Of Horrors	*	TV
Clue	***	TV
The Burbs	*	Video
Big	****	Video
Once Bitten	**	TV
Funny Farm	**	TV
Twins	**	Video
Throw Mama From The Train	*	Video
Frankie And Johnny	**	Video
Peggy Sue Got Married	***	Video
Mannequin	**	Video
BackDraft	****	Video
Tequila Sunrise	**	Video
Lethal Weapon	***	TV
Lethal Weapon 2	***	Video
Coming To America	**	Video
Trading Places	**	Video
The Golden Child	*	Video
Jumping Jack Flash	**	Video
The Lady In White	***	Video
Can't Buy Me Love	***	TV
License To Drive	**	Video
Lucas	**	TV

Like Father, Like Son	**	TV
Bill and Ted's Excellent Adventure	**	Video
Three For The Road	***	Video
Hatchet	***	Video
Witness	***	Video
Parenthood	**	Video
Cocktail	***	Video
Rainman	***	Video
Roadhouse	**	Video
The Hunt For Red October	***	Video
Air America	***	Video
The Abyss	****	Video
Walk Like A Man	**	Video
Second Sight	*	Video
Bachelor Party	***	Video
Fresh Horses	**	Video
She's Having A Baby	***	Video
Little Mermaid	***	Video
The Untouchables	***	Video
Necessary Parties	****	TV
Dirty Dancing	****	Video
Tucker	**	Video
Mosquito Coast	***	Video

D.O.A.	***	TV
Kickboxer	**	Video
Steel Magnolias	****	Video
When Harry Met Sally	****	Video
Beaches	****	Video
Willow	****	Theater
Who Framed Roger Rabbit	***	Video
An American Tale	***	Video
Dead Poet's Society	****	Video
Lampoon's Christmas Vacation	***	Video
Weekend At Bernies	**	Video
The Land Before Time	***	Video
Field Of Dreams	****	Video
Look Who's Talking	***	Video
Mermaids	***	Video

90s Movies

Always	***	Theater
Chances Are	**	Video
Field of Dreams	***	Video
Frantic	***	Video
The Fabulous Baker Boys	**	Video
Awakenings	***	Video
Pretty Woman	***	Theater
Ghost	****	Theater
Sarah Plain and Tall	***	TV
Lantern Hill	***	TV
The Mambo Kings	***	Video
Dances With Wolves	****	Theater
The Fisher King	**	Video
Cadmic Man	*	Video
Don't Tell Her It's Me	**	Video
My Blue Heaven	**	Video
Navy Seals	*	Video
Scandal	**	Video
The Freshman	**	Video
The Family Business	**	Video
Straight Talk	**	Video

Joe Vs The Volcano	**	Theater
Wild At Heart	***	Video
Housesitter	**	Video
He Said, She Said	**	Video
Lord Of The Flies	**	Video
Men At Work	*	Video
Back To The Future 2	**	Theater
Back To The Future 3	***	Theater
Aracnidphobia	**	Video
800 Leagues Down The Amazon	**	Video
Neverending Story 2	**	Theater
Where Sleeping Dogs Lie	**	Video
What About Bob	**	Video
Gremlins 2	*	Video
Who's Harry Crumb	*	Video
Sneakers	***	Video
Dick Tracy	**	Theater
Batman	**	Video
For The Boys	***	Video
Fantasia	***	Theater
Pacific Heights	**	Video
The Prince of Pennsylvania	***	Video
Dead Again	****	Theater

Point Break	***	Drive In
Robin Hood: Prince	***	Theater
Dead Calm	***	Video
My Step-Mother Is An Alien	*	Video
Gross Anatomy	**	Video
Flatliners	***	Video
Brotherhood Of Justice	*	Video
My Girl	***	Theater
Pump Up The Volume	***	Video
My Boyfriend's Back	*	Video
Deceived	**	Theater
Pure Luck	*	Video
Only The Lonely	*	Video
Sibling Rivalry	**	Video
Rambling Rose	**	Video
Man In The Moon	***	Video
Hook	**	Theater
Receiver Dogs	**	Video
Single White Female	**	Video
The Prince Of Tides	****	Theater
Days Of Thunder	***	Video
The Silence Of The Lambs	***	Video
Beauty And The Beast	****	Theater

Crush	**	Video
The Good Son	**	Video
Shinning Through	**	Theater
Class Action	***	Video
The Killing Mind	***	TV
Caroline	**	TV
The Hand That Rocks The Cradle	***	Theater
City Slickers	**	Video
Father Of The Bride	***	Video
Man Trouble	**	Video
Paradise	***	Video
City Of Joy	**	Theater
The Doors	****	Video
Curly Sue	**	Theater
Houseguests	**	Video
Misery	***	Video
Fried Green Tomatoes	***	Theater
Bird On A Wire	***	Video
Narrow Margin	***	Video
The Last Boy Scout	**	Video
Medicine Man	****	Theater
Alibi	*	Video
Mobsters	**	Video

Stella	***	Video
A River Runs Through It	***	Theater
Cool World	**	Video
Cool Runnings	***	Video
Fern Gully	***	Video
Thunderheart	***	Theater
Unlawful Entry	**	Theater
Shattered	**	Video
Far And Away	***	Theater
Death Becomes Her	**	Theater
Rudy	***	Video
A League Of Their Own	***	Theater
Thelma and Louise	***	Video
Driving Miss Daisy	***	Video
Mugsy	**	Video
Another Stakeout	**	Video
Revenge	***	Video
Philadelphia	***	Video
Skylark	***	TV
Might Ducks	*	Theater
The Rocketeer	*	Video
Cuffs	**	Video
Bill and Ted's Bogus Journey	*	Theater

Total Recall	**	Video
Problem Child	*	Theater
Hot Shots	**	Video
Tune In Tomorrow	**	Video
Home Alone	***	Theater
Home Alone 2	**	Theater
The Gun In Betty Lou's Handbag	**	Video
VI Warsharski	**	Video
The Last Action Hero	*	Theater
To The Point Of No Return	***	Video
Regarding Henry	***	Video
Career Opportunities	**	Video
Last Of The Mohicans	**	Theater
Turner And Hooch	**	Video
Angie	***	Video
Dying Young	***	Video
Soap Dish	***	Theater
School Ties	***	Video
This Boy's Life	***	TV
Basic Instinct	***	Theater
Buffy The Vampire Slayer	**	Video
Sister Act	**	Theater
The Bodyguard	**	Theater

Untamed Heart	****	Video
Postcards From The Edge	***	Theater
Final Analysis	***	Video
Red Shoe Diaries	***	Video
Bram Stoker's Dracula	*** *	Theater
Prelude To A Kiss	**	Video
Jennifer 8	**	Video
Traces Of Red	***	Video
Beethoven's 2ed	*	Drive In
Guilty As Sin	**	Video
Wayne's World	**	Drive-In
Adams Family	***	Video
Don't Tell Mom The Babysitter Is Dead	**	Class
Sleepless In Seattle	****	Theater
A Few Good Men	***	Video
Groundhog's Day	*	Theater
Madonna's Truth Or Dare	***	Video
French Kiss	***	Theater
Rush	***	Video
The Power Of One	****	Video
Sommersby	***	Theater
White Wolves II Cry In the Wild	**	Video
Angie	**	Video

Benny And Joon	**	Video
Exit To Eden	**	Video
Look Who's Talking Too	**	Video
The Dreamer Of OZ	***	TV
Sleeping With The Enemy	**	Video
Little Man Tate	***	Video
Guarding Tess	*	Video
Encino Man	**	Video
Cape Fear	*	Video
The Cutting Edge	***	Video
Scissors	*	Video
Sliver	***	Theater
Body Of Evidence	**	Video
White Sands	**	Video
Ernest Scared Stupid	**	Video
Blue Lagoon 2	**	Video
Disclosure	**	Video
Boomerang	**	Video
Malice	**	Theater
Mel Gibson's Hamlet	****	Video
What's Love Got To Do With It	***	Video
Shock'em Dead	*	Video
Reality Bites	***	Video

Harley Davidson and The Malbro Man	**	Video
Candyman	**	Video
Wild Orchid	**	Video
Showgirls	**	Video
Free Willy	*	Video
Scent Of A Woman	***	Video
White Men Can't Jump	***	Video
Newsies	**	Class
Hero	*	Video
The Baby Doll Murders	_	Video
The Crying Game	**	Video
Mad Dog And Glory	*	Video
My Cousin Vinny	***	Video
The Butcher's Wife	*	Video
Leaving Normal	**	Video
Vanished	*	TV
Fearless	**	Video
The Flinstones Movie	**	Video
Greedy	**	TV
Life With Mikey	**	Video
Indecent Proposal	***	Video
Forever Young	***	Video
Ice Runner	****	Video

Blown Away	*	Video
Poison Ivy	**	Video
Hot Shots Part Deux	*	Video
The Secret Garden	***	Video
Aladdin	***	Video
Love Potion #9	**	Video
Whispers In The Dark	**	Video
Poetic Justice	***	Video
Mrs. Doubtfire	***	Theater
Adams Family Values	**	Theater
The Man Without A Face	***	Video
The Temp	**	Video
My Life	**	Video
Waiting To Exhale	**	Video
The Three Little Ninjas	**	Video
So I Married An Ax Murder	**	Video
Fatal Instinct	*	Video
The Firm	***	Theater
Much Ado About Nothing	***	Video
The Crow	****	Theater
The Professional	***	TV
With Honors	***	Video
The Lion King	***	Theater

Damage	****	Video
The Color Of Night	**	Theater
When A Man Loves A Woman	****	Theater
Cliffhanger	**	Video
The Specialist	*	Video
Immortal Beloved	**	Video
Natural Born Killers	**	Theater
Drop Dead Fred	***	Video
Sleepwalkers	**	Video
Passion Fish	***	Video
Mr. Saturday Night	*	Video
A Time To Kill	**	Video
Mississippi Burning	**	Class
River Wild	**	Video
Before Sunrise	***	Video
Dumb and Dumber	***	Theater
A Stranger Among Us	***	Video
Only You	**	Theater
Time Cop	**	Theater
Love Affair	**	Video
Hide Away	**	Theater
The Rising Sun	***	Video
Ritchie Rich	*	Theater

Now and Then	***	Video
Junior	*	Theater
Interview With A Vampire	****	Theater
Rob Roy	***	Video
Speed	***	Theater
Safe Passage	***	Video
Forest Gump	****	Theater
Ace Ventura: Pet Detective	***	Video
Terminal Velocity	*	Video
True Lies	**	Theater
Frankenstien	***	Theater
Age Of Innocence	***	Video
Stargate	***	Theater
Intersection	**	Video
Chasers	*	Video
Kindergarten Cop	*	Video
Grumpy Old Men	***	Video
The Mask	**	Video
Speechless	**	Theater
Four Weddings And A Funeral	***	Video
City Slickers 2	**	Video
Mrs. Rose White	**	Video
Being Human	**	Video

Consenting Adults	***	TV
Glass Menagerie	***	Video
Nell	****	Theater
Blink	***	Video
The Scarlet Letter	**	Video
The Three Musketeers	**	Video
Blaze	*	Video
Bad Boys	**	Theater
Schindler's List	***	Video
Boys On The Side	**	Video
The Paper	*	Video
Nothing But Trouble	*	Video
I'll Do Anything	*	Video
Sid And Nancy	**	Video
What's Eating Gilbert Grape	***	Video
Jason's Lyric	***	Video
Mad Love	***	Theater
Forget Paris	***	Theater
Mrs. Parker And The Vicious Circle	***	Video
Braveheart	****	Theater
Love and A .45	***	Video
Don Juan De Marco	***	Video
Shadowlands	***	Video

Trial By Jury	**	Video
The Juror	**	Video
First Knight	**	Theater
The Sandlot	**	Video
The Little Rascals	***	Video
Angles In The Outfield	**	Video
A Walk In The Clouds	**	Theater
IQ	*	Video
Billy Madison	**	Video
Major Payne	**	Video
Coneheads	*	Video
Desperado	**	Video
Break Down	**	Video
Flesh and Bone	***	Video
Seven	***	Theater
Clerks	****	Video
Dangerous Minds	***	Theater
Pulp Fiction	*** Video	
Legends Of The Fall	****	Theater
Murder In The First	***	Video
Kalifornia	**	Video
The Shawshank Redemption	***	Video
Jurassic Park	**	Video

Apollo 13	***	Video
Bed Of Roses	***	Theater
Three of Hearts	**	Video
A Pyromaniac's Love Story	*	Video
True Romance	***	Video
Waterworld	**	Video
Too Young To Die	**	Video
Born Yesterday	**	Video
Kids	**	Video
The Englishman Who	*	Video
Basketball Diaries	***	Video
Jungle To Jungle	**	Theater
Strange Days	***	Video
Beyond Rangoon	***	Video
Threesome	**	Video
Fatherhood	*	Video
The Birdcage	**	Theater
Little Women	***	Video
How To Make An American Quilt	***	Video
Up Close And Personal	*	Video
To Die For	**	Video
Down Periscope	*	Theater
Sgt. Bilko	**	Video

Before And After	***	Video
Virtuosity	***	Video
Hackers	****	Video
To Gillian On Her 37th Birthday	**	Video
Broken Arrow	**	Theater
A Vampire In Brooklyn	*	Video
The Money Train	***	Video
The Cowboy Way	***	Video
Demolition Man	***	Video
Jack	**	Video
Jury Duty	*	Video
A Perfect World	***	Video
No Escape	**	Video
Never Talk To Strangers	***	Video
Jumanji	**	Video
Diabloique	**	Video
Unforgettable	***	Video
Toy Story	****	Theater
White Squall	***	Video
Dolores Clayborn	***	Video
Black Sheep	*	Video
Made In America	**	Video
The Client	***	Video

Nutty Professor	**	Video
Home For The Holiday	***	Theater
Bio-Dome	*	Video
Dave	**	Video
National Lampoon's Loaded Weapon	*	Video
The American President	**	Video
The Net	**	Video
The Real McCoy	**	Video
Milk Money	**	Video
Get Shorty	**	Video
Sabrina	**	Theater
Casino	***	Video
Fools Rush In	**	Video
The Last Seduction	***	Video
Bridges Of Madison Co.	**	Theater
Johnny Mnemonic	**	Video
Four Rooms	***	Video
Babe	**	Video
Striptease	**	Video
Dante's Peak	*	Video
Volcano	**	Video
Sense and Sensibility	***	Video
Lord Of Illusions	**	Video

The Arrival	***	Video
Flirting With Disaster	***	Video
Sleepers	**	Video
Spy Hard	**	Video
Mary Riely	**	Video
Jade	**	Video
12 Monkeys	***	Theater
Speed 2	**	Video
Wild Orchid 2: Two Shade Of Blue	***	Video
A Very Brady Movie	**	Video
Wrongfully Accused	**	Video
Crimson Tide	***	Video
Fair Game	**	Video
Species	**	Video
The Craft	*	Theater
Nick Of Time	***	Video
Copycat	***	Video
Tombstone	***	Video
The Last Dance	**	Video
Once Were Warriors	****	Video
Phenomenon	****	Theater
Dragonheart	**	Video
Eraser	**	Video

Beautiful Girls	***	Video
Circle Of Friends	***	Video
Set It Off	****	Video
Face/Off	***	Video
Passenger 57	***	Video
Multiplicity	*	Video
The Devil's Own	**	Video
The Fugitive	***	Video
From Dusk Until Dawn	**	Video
Twister	***	Drive-In
The Usual Suspects	***	Video
King Pin	*	Video
A Rumble In The Bronx (Jackie Chan)	**	Video
It Could Happen To You	**	Video
The Joy Luck Club	***	Video
Tank Girl	**	Video
Powder	***	Theater
Something To Talk About	**	Video
Ace Ventura 2	**	Video
Trial And Error	**	Video
Mission Impossible	***	Video
Independence Day	**	Theater
Leaving Las Vegas	**	Video

Tin Cup	*	Video
Men In Black	***	Theater
Romeo + Juliet	***	Theater
Waterboy	*	Theater
The People Vs Larry Flint	***	Video
Jerry McGuire	***	Video
Robin Hood: Men In Tights	**	Video
Crow 2: City Of Angels	**	Video
Dracula: Dead And Loving It	*	Video
Chain Reaction	*	Video
The Associate	**	Video
Metro	**	Video
The Saint	***	Theater
In Love And War	**	Video
Courage Under Fire	***	Video
Emma	***	Video
High School High	**	Video
Beverly Hills Ninja	*	Video
Tommy Boy	*	Video
The Stoned Age	**	Video
Beavis and Butthead	**	Theater
Clueless	***	Video
Kansas City	***	Video

A Thing Called Love	**	Video
Like Water For Chocolate	***	Video
The Story Of O	**	Video
Liar, Liar	***	Theater
I Love You To Death	***	Video
The House Of The Spirits	***	Video
Moonlight and Valentino	**	Video
Feeling Minnesota	***	Video
Fargo	*	Video
Floundering	*	Video
Exoctica	*	Video
Six Degrees Of Separation	**	Video
Marvin's Room	**	Video
The Quick And The Dead	**	Video
Half Baked	**	Video
Police Story (Jackie Chan)	**	Video
The Fifth Element	***	Video
The First Wives Club	**	Video
Trainspotting	**	Video
The Wedding Singer	***	Video
9 Months	**	Video
Anastasia	***	Theater
The Matchmaker	*	Video

In And Out	*	Video
Air Force One	**	Video
Devil's Advocate	***	Video
Absolute Power	***	Video
The Brothers McMullan	***	Video
She's The One	**	Video
A Night At The Roxberry	*	Theater
Muriel's Wedding	***	Video
Two If By Sea	**	Video
Gross Point Blank	**	Video
Breaking The Waves	*	Video
Slingblade	*	Video
Addicted To Love	**	Theater
The Long Kiss Goodnight	***	Video
Austin Powers 2	**	Video
The Ghost In The Darkness	***	Video
Scream	**	Video
Father's Day	*	Video
The Cable Guy	**	Video
Space Jam	**	Video
Secrets and Lies	**	Class
Michael	**	Video
The New Age	*	Video

The Full Monty	**	Video
Flubber	***	Video
Extreme Measures	**	Video
The Rock	***	Video
Midnight In The Garden Of Good And Evil	*	Video
Mr. Holland's Opus	***	Video
The English Patient	***	Video
Hope Floats	***	Video
My Giant	**	Video
The Edge	***	Video
Primal Fear	***	Video
GI Jane	**	Video
Bullworth	***	Video
First Strike (Jackie Chan)	**	Video
Con Air	**	Video
My Best Friend's Wedding	**	Video
Evita	*	Video
Chasing Amy	***	Video
Romey & Michelle's High School Reunion	**	Video
The Jackal	***	Video
Men In Black	***	Video
Contact	****	Video
Conspiracy Theory	***	Video

Les Miserable	*	Video
Hush	**	Video
Great Expectations	**	Video
Good Will Hunting	*****	Theater
Gattica	***	Video
Elizabeth	****	Video
Evening Star	**	Video
Nothing To Lose	***	Video
There is Something About Mary	***	Theater
Even Horizon	*	Video
Wild Things	**	Video
1000 acres	***	Video
Sphere	**	Video
A Perfect Murder	***	Video
U-Turn	**	Video
Selena	***	Video
LA Confidential	**	Video
Seven Years In Tibet	**	Video
Red Corner	***	Video
Boogie Nights	**	Video
2 Days In The Valley	**	Video
Excess Baggage	**	Video
Picture Perfect	**	Video

At First Sight	***	Video
Kripendorf's Tribe	**	Video
Can't Hardly Wait	***	Video
Twilight	***	Theater
How Stella Got Her Groove Back	**	Video
As Good As It Gets	***	Video
Beloved	*	Video
Mercury Rising	***	Video
Armageddon	**	Video
Dead Man On Campus	**	Video
Senseless	**	Video
Six Days, Seven Nights	**	Video
Titanic	***	Video
Ever After	****	Theater
Stealing Beauty	****	Video
Mulan	***	Video
Soul Food	***	Video
Wuthering Heights 1992	****	Video
The Kama Sutra	***	Video
Belle De Jour	**	Video
Wings of The Dove	***	Video
You've Got Mail	***	Theater
My Family	***	Class

Gia	***	Video
Replacement Killers	***	Video
Playing God	***	Video
Forces Of Nature	**	Video
Wag The Dog	**	Video
Fear And Loathing In Las Vegas	**	Video
The Game	***	Video
The X-Files Movie	***	Theater
City Of Angles	***	Video
Wings Of Desire (German) 1989	****	Video
What Dreams May Come	***	Video
One True Thing	***	Video
Mr. Nice Guy	**	Video
The Avengers	*	Video
Mighty Joe Young	***	Video
Foxfire	***	Video
A Bug's Life	***	Video
Antz	***	Video
Primary Colors	*	Video
Man In The Iron Mask	*	Video
The Mask Of Zorro	***	Video
Lolita	***	Video
Big Daddy	**	Video

Step-Mom	***	Video
Payback	**	Video
US Marshals	***	Video
Tomorrow Never Dies	**	Video
Dreams (Japanese)	***	Video
Enemy Of The State	***	Video
Message In A Bottle	**	Video
Blue (French)	***	Video
Kiss The Girls	***	Video
For Richer Or Poorer	**	Theater
Practical Magic	***	Video
Blade	***	Video
The Opposite Of Sex	****	Video
The Matrix	****	Theater
Dark City	****	Video
Dangerous Beauty	****	Video
Henry and June	****	Video
Shakespeare In Love	****	Video
Star Wars: Episode I	***	Theater
The Horse Whisperer	***	Video
The Truman Show	***	Video
The 13th Warrior	**	Video
Godzilla 1999	*	Video

Go	**	Video
The Haunting	**	Drive-In
Apt Pupil	***	Video
200 Cigarettes	***	Video
Patch Adams	***	Video
Out Of Sight	***	Video
Austin Powers 3	**	Video
Rounders	**	Video
The Rainmaker	***	Video
Nottinghill	***	Video
Rush Hour	***	Video
Wild Wild West	**	Video
Toy Story 2	***	Theater
Pleasantville	***	Video
The Prince Of Egypt	**	Video
Palmetto	**	Video
The Mod Squad	**	Video
The Story Of Us	***	Video
Random Hearts	**	Video
Eyes Wide Shut	**	Video
The Out Of Towners	**	Video
Office Space	**	Video
Star Trek: Insurrection	***	Video

Very Bad Things	**	Video
Ed TV	**	Video
Entrapment	***	Video
The 13th Floor	***	Video
The Bone Collector	***	Video
Cruel Intentions	***	Video
Dogma	***	Theater
The Mummy	***	Video
The Sixth Sense	***	Video
The Red Violin	****	Video

2000 Movies

Girl Interrupted	***	Theater
Where The Heart Is	***	Theater
Anywhere But Here	**	Video
The End Of The Affair	****	Video
The Runaway Bride	**	Video
Snow Falling On Cedars	***	Video
American Pie	**	Video
American Beauty	***	Video
Hurricane	***	Theater
Never Been Kissed	**	Video
Galaxy Quest	***	Video
Three To Tango	**	Video
Detroit Rock	**	Video
Inspector Gadget	**	Video
Analyze This	**	Video
Shanghai Noon	**	Theater
Gun Shy	*	Video
Mission Impossible 2	***	Theater
The World Is Not Enough	**	Video
The Thomas Crown Affair	**	Video
Double Jeopardy	**	Video

Title	Rating	Format
Me, Myself and Irene	**	Theater
The Green Mile	***	Video
Sleepy Hollow	***	Video
Bless The Child	**	Theater
The Beach	***	Video
Drowning Mona	***	Video
Simple Irresistible	**	Video
Unbearable Lightness	***	Video
Playing By Heart	****	Video
Desert Blue	***	Video
Man On The Moon	**	Video
Romeo Must Die	**	Video
Here On Earth	**	Video
28 Days	***	Video
Anna And The King	***	Video
The Next Best Thing	**	Video
The Very Thought Of You	***	Video
Duce Bigalo	*	Video
Bringing Out The Dead	**	Video
U-571	***	Video
Erin Brockovich	***	Video
High Fidelity	***	Video
Keeping The Faith	***	Video

Unbreakable	***	Video
Scary Movie	**	Video
True Story of Vlad	**	TV
Family Man	***	Theater
The Patriot	***	Video
Gladiator	***	Video
Chicken Run	**	Video
Gone In 60 Seconds	**	Video
Center Stage	**	Video
Return To Me	***	Video
Empire Records (1995)	**	Video
Groove	***	Video
Saving Grace	***	Video
Delta of Venus (1992)	**	Video
The Virgin Suicides	****	Video
Mission To Mars	***	Video
Dangerous Liaisons (1988)	****	Video
What Lies Beneath	***	Video
Defending Your Life (1990)	***	Video
Bedazzled	***	Video
Dune	****	Video
China Moon (1989)	**	Video
Amy and Isabelle	***	TV

Pushing Tin	***	Video
Fire (1998)	**	Video
Meet The Parents	***	Video
Almost Famous	****	Video
Charlie's Angels	***	Video
Young Frankenstien	***	TV
The Polish Wedding	****	TV
Hamlet (2000)	***	Video
Finding Forrester	****	Video
Boys and Girls	****	Video
Bounce	***	Video
A Knight's Tale	****	Theater
What Women Want	***	Plane
Legend Of Bagger Vance	*	Plane
13 Days	*	Plane
Shrek	****	Theater
Committed	***	Video
Traffic	***	Video
Crouching Tiger	****	Video
Tomb Raider	***	Theater
Shadow of the Vampire	**	Video
Oh Brother Where Art Thou	***	Video
Miss Congeniality	***	Video

Save the Last Dance	****	Video
The House of Mirth	***	Video
Castaway	****	Video
Red Planet	**	Video
The Wedding Planner	***	Video
Princess Mononoke	***	Video
The Mists of Avalon	****	TV
Saving Silverman	**	Video
Sweet November	***	Video
Legally Blond	***	Theater
Titus	***	Video
Nurse Betty	**	Video
Wildflower	***	Video
Rush Hour 2	***	Theater
Josie and the Pussy Cats	***	Video
Dungeons and Dragons	**	Video
The Gift	***	Video
Head Over Heels	***	Video
Waking The Dead	***	Video
Women and Men (1990)	***	Video
Coyote Ugly	**	Video
American Pie 2	**	Theater
Jay and Silent Bob	***	Theater

The Rapture (1991)	*	Video
The Mummy Returns	***	Video
Glitter	***	Theater
Bridget Jones's Diary	***	Video
Down To You	***	Video
Spy Kids	***	Video
Cats and Dogs	**	PPV
One Night At McCool's	***	Video
About Adam	***	Video
America's Sweethearts	***	Video
Lord of the Rings	*****	Theater
Pearl Harbor	***	Video
Moulin Rouge	***	Video
Evolution	**	Video
The Fast and the Furious	***	Video
Dude Where's My Car	**	Video
Atlantis	***	Video
Inventing the Abbotts	***	TV
What's the Worst…?	***	Video
Princess Diaries	***	Video
Don't Say A Word	***	Video
Ghost World	***	Video
Harry Potter	***	Theater

Movies Seen 2003-2004

Black Knight	**	HBO
Spirited Away	***	DVD
Count of Monte Cristo	***	DVD
Big Fat Liar	***	DVD
Matrix Reloaded	*****	Theatre
Kissing Jessica Stein	***	DVD
One Hour Photo	**	DVD
Analyze That	***	DVD
The Hours	***	DVD
Frieda	***	DVD
Phonebooth	**	Video
Gangs of NY	***	DVD
How To Lose A Guy In Ten Days	***	DVD
Bruce Almighty	****	Theatre
The Majestic	***	HBO
Shanghai Knights	***	DVD
The Life of David Gale	****	DVD
Bringing Down The House	***	DVD
What A Girl Wants	***	DVD
Chicago	**	DVD
2 Fast 2 Furious	**	DVD
View From The Top	**	DVD
Daddy Daycare	***	DVD
Down With Love	**	DVD
The In Laws	**	DVD
Hollywood Homicide	**	DVD
Charlie's Angles: Full Throttle	**	DVD

Title	Year	Rating	Format
Bend It Like Beckam		***	DVD
LOTR: Return of The King		****	Theatre
Finding Nemo		****	DVD
The Transportor		***	HBO
Dumber and Dumberer		**	DVD
Underworld		**	DVD
Alex and Emma		***	DVD
Amy's O	2000	***	Video
Stir of Echoes	2000	**	TV
Life is Beautiful	2001	**	Video
Restoration	1998	*	Video
Family Pictures	1990	**	TV
Slidding Doors	1999	***	Video
Hanging Up	2000	**	Video
Serving Sara	2002	**	Video
Enemy At Gates	2003	*	Video
Mr. Ripley	2001	*	Video
Loser	2000	***	Video
Kate and Leopold	2003	*	DVD
Autumn in NY	2002	*	Video
Road to Perdition	2003	**	Video
Dragonfly	2003	***	DVD
Monan's Spring	1986	**	DVD
Changing Lanes	2002	**	Video
Simone	2002	**	Video
Three Kings	1999	*	Video
Duets	1998	*	Video
Under The Tuscan Sun		***	Video
Man Who Wasn't	2001	*	Video
General's Daughter		***	Video
Signs	2001	*	Video

Uptown Girls	2003	***	DVD
Say It Isn't So	2001	*	Video
Zoolander	2001	**	DVD
Tuck Everlasting	2002	***	Video
Heartbreakers	2001	*	Video
Scorpion King	2002	**	DVD
Angela's Ashe	2000	**	Video
Annie Hall	1977	**	DVD
My Dog Skip	1999	*	DVD
SNG: Nemsis	2002	*	DVD
The Good Girl	2002	***	Video
Magnolia	2000	**	Video
Anne of Green 3	2000	*	Video
Titan A.E.	2000	***	Video
I Am Sam	2002	***	DVD
Cider House	2001	***	Video
The Cell	2000	***	Video
Whale Rider	2003	***	Video
Monsoon Wed	2001	*	Video
The Piano	2000	**	Video
Iris	2002	***	Video
The Medallion	2002	*	Video
The Recruit	2003	***	DVD
Far From Heaven	2003	***	Video
Lost In Translation	2003	***	DVD
Divorce	2003	***	DVD
Pumpkin	2001	***	Video
Intolerable Cruelty	2003	**	DVD
Pieces of April	2003	***	DVD
Miss Tingle	1999	**	Video
Fight Club	1999	***	Video

Truth About Charlie	2003		Video
Sylvia	2003	****	DVD
Matrix Revolutions	2003	***	DVD
Something's Gotta	2003	***	DVD
About Schmidt	2003		DVD
How To Deal	2003	***	DVD
Master and Com	2003		DVD
Identity	2003	***	DVD
Matchstick Men	2003	***	DVD
Wonder Boys	2002	***	Video
13 Going On 30	2004	****	Theatre
Cheaper By The Dozen		***	DVD
Brother Bear	2003	***	DVD
Sinbad	2003	***	DVD
The Last Samurai		****	DVD
Scary Movie 3		***	DVD
Love Actually		***	DVD
Big Fish		**	DVD
Paycheck		***	DVD
Cat In The Hat		***	Video
Thirteen		****	DVD
Girl Pearl Earring		***	DVD
The Missing	2004	***	
In The Cut		***	
Kill Bill		****	
Gigli		*	
Freaky Friday			

Movies Seen 2004 and 2005

Against The Ropes	2004	**	DVD	
Raising Helen	2004	***	DVD	
Prisoner of Azkaban	2004	*****	DVD	
Healing Yoga	2000	***	DVD	Dec-04
Pollack	2004	***	DVD	
The Whole 9 YDS	2000	***	Video	
The Whole 10 YRDS	2004	**	Video	
The Alamo	2003	*	Video	
Chasing Liberty	2004	**	DVD	
The Perfect Score	2004	**	DVD	
The Passion	2004	*****	DVD	
Monster	2004	***	DVD	Jan-05
LOTR Nat'L Geo	2004	***	DVD	
Head of State	2004	**	Video	
The Secret Window	2004	**	DVD	
Envy	2004	*	DVD	
Day After Tomorrow	2004	***	DVD	
The Forgotten	2004	***	DVD	
Sky Captain	2004	***	DVD	
Garden State	2004	***	DVD	
Taxi	2004	**	DVD	
Sex in The City S2V2	2002	***	DVD	
Sex In the City S3V1	2002	***	DVD	
Shark Tale	2004	***	DVD	
The Incredibles	2004	***	DVD	Mar-05
Collateral	2004	***	DVD	
Unfortunate Events	2005	***	Theatre	

Title	Year	Rating	Format	Date
Scooby Doo 2	2004	***	DVD	
Closer	2004	****	DVD	May-05
Revenge of The Sith	2005	****	Theatre	
National Treasure	2005	***	DVD	
The Aviator	2005	**	DVD	
In Good Company	2005	***	DVD	
Hitch	2005	***	DVD	
I, Robot	2005	****	DVD	Jul-05
Miss Congeniality 2	2005	***	DVD	
I Heart Hucklebees	2004	***	DVD	
The Upside Of Anger	2005	***	DVD	
Million Dollar Baby	2005	***	DVD	
The Little Black Book	2005	***	DVD	
Everybody's Famous	2000	***	DVD	
We Don't Live Here Anymore		****	DVD	
Alfie	2004	***	Video	
Daddy and Them	2004	**	Video	
Be Cool	2005	***	Video	
Sin City	2005	***	DVD	
Sex In The City S1V1		***	DVD	
Sex In The City S1V2		***	DVD	
Sex In The City S2V1		***	DVD	
Sex In The City S6V3		***	DVD	
Sitch Has A Glitch	2005	***	DVD	
Ray	2004	****	HBO	
Hitchhikers Guide	2005	****	DVD	
Cellular	2005	***	DVD	
Sex In The City S4V1		***	DVD	
Sex in the City S4V2		***	DVD	
Sex In the City S4V3		***	DVD	
Smile	2005	**	DVD	Oct-05

Robots	2005	***	DVD	
Sideways	2005	*	DVD	Nov-05
HP: Goblet Of Fire	2005	****	Theatre	
Sahara	2005	***	DVD	
Chocolate Factory	2005	**	DVD	
Madagascar	2005	***	DVD	
Princess Diaries 2	2004	***	DVD	Dec-05
Dukes of Hazard	2005	**	DVD	
Mr. &Mrs. Smith	2005	***	DVD	
The Island	2005	***	DVD	Jan-06
The Polar Express	2005	***	DVD	
The Wedding Crashers	2005	**	DVD	
The Wedding Date	2005	***	DVD	Feb-06
Prozac Nation	2005	***	DVD	
Spanglish	2005	***	DVD	
Proof	2005	****	DVD	
In Her Shoes	2005	***	DVD	
Just Like Heaven	2005	***	DVD	Mar-06
Corpse Bride	2005	***	DVD	
War of the Worlds	2005	***	DVD	
Shopgirl	2005	****	Theatre	
Kathy Smith Yoga			DVD	
Batman Begins	2005	****	DVD	
Memoirs of a Geisha	2005	***	DVD	Apr-06
A History of Violence	2005	***	DVD	
A Lot Like Love	2005	**	DVD	
Lion, Witch Wardrobe	2005	****	DVD	
Watership Down	1977	**	Video	
Christmas Kranks	2005	*	DVD	May-06
Paparazzi	2005	**	DVD	
Brother's Grimm	2005	***	DVD	

Tristian and Isolde	2005	***	DVD	
Electra	2004	***	DVD	Jun-06
Alexander	2005	**	DVD	
Kingdom of Heaven	2005		DVD	
Must Love Dogs	2005	***	DVD	
Rumor Has It	2005	***	DVD	
Failure To Launch	2006	***	DVD	Sep-06
Firewall	2006	**	DVD	
Racing Stripes	2006	**	DVD	
Walk The Line	2005	***	DVD	
Notorious	1946	****	DVD	Oct-06
Over the Hedge	2006	****	DVD	
Cars	2006	***	DVD	Nov-06
Casanova	2006	***	DVD	
The Family Stone	2006	****	DVD	
Syriana	2006	**	DVD	
Lucky # Sleven	2006	***	DVD	
The Da Vinci Code	2006	****	DVD	
North By Northwest	1956	****	DVD	
To Catch A Thief	1958	***	DVD	Dec-06
Take The Lead	2006	***	DVD	
The Break-Up	2006	***	DVD	
Tokoyo Drift	2006	*	DVD	
Dead Man's Chest	2006	***	DVD	
V For Vendetta	2006	****	DVD	
Clerks 2	2006	**	DVD	Jan-07
Scary Movie 4	2006	**	DVD	
Barnyard	2006	***	DVD	
Superman Returns	2006	***	DVD	
Epic Movie	2007	**	Theatre	
Date Movie	2006	**	DVD	Feb-07

Title	Year	Rating	Format	Date
The Illusionist	2006	****	DVD	
She's The Man	2006	***	DVD	
Marie Antoinette	2006	***	DVD	
Hoodwinked	2006	****	DVD	
Open Season	2006	***	DVD	
Little Miss Sunshine	2006	****	DVD	Apr-07
Click	2006	***	DVD	
RV	2006	**	DVD	
IA2 The Melt Down	2006	***	DVD	
Thnk U 4 Smoking	2006	***	DVD	Jun-07
Devil Wears Prada	2006	***	DVD	
Black Dahlia	2006	***	DVD	
Eragon	2006	***	DVD	
Music and Lyrics	2007	***	DVD	
The Holiday	2007	***	DVD	
The Good Shepherd	2006	***	DVD	
My Super ExGirlfriend	2006	**	DVD	Jul-07
Happy Feet	2006	**	DVD	
March of The Peguins	2006	**	DVD	
At The Lake House	2006	***	DVD	
HP Order of Phoenix	2007	*****	Theatre	
Dejvu	2007	****	DVD	
Skeleton Key	2006	***	DVD	Aug-07
Sherry Baby	2006	***	DVD	
Shrek the Third	2007	***	Theatre	
Happily Never After	2007	**	DVD	
Charleotte's Web	2007	***	DVD	
Catch and Release	2007	****	DVD	Sep-07
The Last Kiss	2007	****	DVD	
The Simpsons Movie	2007	****	Theatre	
Surf's Up	2007	***	DVD	

Casino Royal	2007	**	DVD	Nov-07
The Fountain	2006	**	DVD	
Eastern Promises	2007	****	DVD	Mar-08
Waitress	2007	****	DVD	
Repo Man	1984	**	Video	
Xanadu	1980	*	Video	May-08
Kingdom Crystal Skull	2008	****	Theatre	
The Golden Compass	2007	***	DVD	Jun-08
The Nanny Diaries	2007	***	DVD	
Beaowulf	2007	***	DVD	Jul-08
Books of Secrets	2007	**	DVD	
Definitely, Maybe	2007	****	DVD	
Charlie Wilson's War	2007	****	DVD	
Enchanted	2007	****	DVD	
Knocked Up	2007	****	DVD	Aug-08
27 Dresses	2008	***	DVD	
Rush Hour 3	2007	***	DVD	
Juno	2008	****	DVD	
Vantage Point	2008	****	DVD	
Meet the Robinsons	2007	***	DVD	
The Bee Movie	2008	***	DVD	
Kung Fu Panda	2008	***	Computer	
Atonement	2008	****	DVD	
Premonition	2006	***	DVD	
Sex & The City Movie	2008	***	DVD	
Fahrenheit 451	1968	**	DVD	
Shape of Things	1938	**	DVD	
Tinkerbell	2008	***	Computer	
Bucket List	2008	****	DVD	
Fool's Gold	2008	***	DVD	
Nancy Drew	2008	***	DVD	

Half Blood Prince	Stream	****	Dec-09
Watchmen	Stream	****	
Star Trek	Stream	****	
The Ugly Truth	Stream	***	
He's Just Not That Into You	Stream	***	
Hannah Montana Movie	Netflix	***	
Nick and Norah's Infinite Playlist	Netflix	***	
Up	Netflix	***	
Night at the Museum 2	Netflix	***	
Get Smart	Netflix	***	Jan-10
Angles and Demons	Netflix	***	
The Other Bolyen Girl	Netflix	*****	
A Scanner Darkly	Netflix	***	
Confessions of a Shopoholic	Netflix	***	
Bridewars	Netflix	***	
500 Days of Summer	Netflix	****	
Revolutionary Road	Netflix	****	
Julie and Julia	Netflix	***	
The Curious Case of Benjamin	Netflix	****	
The Changling	Netflix	****	
New In Town	Netflix	***	Feb-10
Away We Go	Netflix	*****	
Valkyrie	Netflix	*****	
Dupicity	Netflix	**	

Downloading

Nancy	Netflix	***
Little Children	Netflix	***
Burn After		
Reading	Netflix	**
Doubt	Netflix	*****
Elizabeth The Golden Age	Netflix	
Phoebe in Wonderland	Netflix	
Black Pearl	Netflix	
Clash of the Titans	Netflix	
The Back-Up Plan	Netflix	
Alice in Wonderland	Netflix	
Bellydance: Arms and Abs	Netflix	
Bellydance: Slim Down	Netflix	
Prince of Persia	Netflix	
Yoga Booty Ballet	Netflix	
Percy Jackson Lightening	Netflix	
Up In the Air	Netflix	
Valentine's Day	Netflix	
Speed Racer	Netflix	
The Lovely Bones	Netflix	
The Princess and the Frog	Netflix	
Fame Remake	Netflix	
Chipmunks: Squeakquel	Netflix	
Ninja	Netflix	
Sherlock Holmes	Netflix	
It's Complicated	Netflix	
Avatar	Netflix	
Couple's Retreat	Netflix	
Love Happens	Netflix	
Saving Face	Netflix	

Imagine Me and You	Netflix
I Can't Think Straight	Netflix
Secretary	Netflix
Breaking and Entering	Netflix
Lions for Lambs	Netflix
Tinker Bell Lost Treasure	Netflix
Transformers	Netflix
Transformers: Fallen	Netflix
Coraline	Netflix
Earthsea	Netflix
Planet 51	Netflix
Did You Hear About Morgan	Netflix
9	Netflix
Hangover	Netflix
Twilight	Netflix
Time Traveler's Wife	Netflix
Eagle Eye	Netflix
Cloudy With Meatballs	Netflix
Star Trek	Netflix
Elizabeth: The Golden Age	Netflix
Burn After Reading	Netflix
Winx Club Season 1	Netflix

Movies From The Library
2011

Brothers and Sisters Season 4

Snowflower and the Secret Fan

Adventure Land

Purple Violets

Candy

My Blueberry Nights

Young Victoria

Waiting

The International

Cars 2

Harry Potter and the Deathly Hallows Part 1

Something Borrowed

The Last Word

Going the Distance

Gigantic

In Her Skin

Super

The Librarian Curse of the Jade Chalice

The Librarian King Solomon's Mines

The Librarian the Spear of Destiny

Life as We Know It

My Best Friend's Girlfriend

Code 46

The Restless

Your Highness

Paul

10 Inch Hero

Sunshine Cleaning

Camille

Taking of Pelham 123

Just Friends

Come Early Morning

Harry Potter Deathly Hallow 2

The Tin Man

Alice

Henry's Crime

Unstoppable

Unknown

Poetry Shi

The Ninth Gate

City of Ember

Inkheart

True Blood Season 1

True Blood Season 2

The Last Time I committed Suicide

Please Give

The Book of Eli

Smart People

I Could Never Be Your Woman

New Scooby Doo Movies Discs 1-4

Barbie: A Fairy Secret

Heavenly Creatures (1997)

Blue Valentine

Billy Blanks Total Fat Blaster

The Other Woman

Harry Potter and the Deathly Hallows Part 1

Narnia: The Voyage of the Dawn Treader

Little Fockers

The Jane Austin Book Club

Serious Moonlight

The Girl Who Kicked The Hornet's Nest (Swedish)

The Social Network

Easy A

Legend of the Guardians

Kim Possible: Stitch in Time

Barbie Mermaidia

Salt

Despicable Me

Inception

The A-Team

Knight and Day

How To Train Your Dragon

Black Swan

How Do You Know?

The Tourist

Love and Suicide

Hereafter

Love and Other Drugs

Beverly Hills Chihuahua

Burlesque

Tangled

Eat, Prey, Love

The Kids Are All Right

Tinker Bell Fairy Rescue

Ramona and Beezus

Shrek Forever After

Sex and the City Movie 2

Date Night

The Karate Kid (Remake)

Smart People

Dedication

The Forbidden Kingdom

Next

The Ghost Writer

Fair Game

Agora

Red

Cracks   (Netflix)

Green Lantern

Cars 2

Wrecked

The Machinist

Hanna

HappyThankYouMorePlease

Bad Teacher

Rio

Thor

Fringe Season 2

The Vampire Diaries Season 2

The Game

The Green Hornet

Beastly

The Tsunami Warrior

The Vampire Effect

The Vampire's Assistant

Vampires Suck

Underworld Revolution

Underworld Rise of the Lycans

Death at a Funeral

Dinner For Smucks

Letters To Juliet

The Lincoln Lawyer   (Netflix)

The Switch

Diary of a Wimpy Kid: Roderick Rules

Gnomeo and Juliet

The Adjustment Bureau

Trust

Grown Ups

Just Go With It

Kickass

Teenage Dirtbag

Suckerpunch

Source Code

Rango

Hall Pass

Red Riding-hood

Pillars of the Earth

Movies 2012

Warehouse 13 S1

Warehouse 13 S2

Warehouse 13 S3

Suburban Girl

Role Models

Spread

Extract

Carolina

Adam

The Post-Grad

The Runaways

Hidalgo (Again)

A History of Violence (Again)

Original Sin (Again)

Shoot 'Em Up

Domino

Caprica

All I Want

Adventureland

The Debt

Castle S1

Castle S2

Castle S3

Brothers and Sisters S5

Reclaiming the Blade

Captain Alatriste

Appaloosa

Saving Grace S1

Saving Grace S2

Saving Grace S3

Bones S6

Charlie Bartlet

Amelia

Babylon 5: Rangers

Babylon 5: Lost Tales

Battlestar Galactica: Razor

Friends with Benefits

Mad Men S1

Mad Men S2

Mad Men S3

Raising Arizona

The Piano (Again)

Home For The Holidays (Again)

Pirates of the Caribbean Stranger Tides

Aurora Borealis

Stone Angel

Wake

Marco Polo

Mad Men S4

Grey's Anatomy S7

The Tournament

Rules of Attraction

Six Wives of Henry

2013

The Hobbit: Unexpected Journey

The Sessions

Parental Guidance

Argo

Cloud Atlas

Moonrise Kingdom

Zero Dark Thirty

Seven Psychopaths

Django Unchained

CSI Miami: Final Season

Grounded For Life

Malcolm in the Middle

Guilt Trip

Silver Linings Playbook

Up All Night Season 1

Warm Bodies

Lincoln

The Great and Powerful Oz

Beasts of the Southern Wild

Samantha Who Season 1 and 2

True Blood Season 5

Jack Reacher

Covert Affairs Season 3

Futurama Seasons 5 and 7

The Life of Pi

CSI NY: The Final Season

Fringe Season 4

2 Broke Girls Season 1

Our Idiot Brother

50/50

Happy Ending Season 1 and 2

Pushing Daisies

24 Season 7and Season 8

Butter

Oblivion

The Usual Suspects (Again)

The Pill

Hysteria

Beware the Gonzo

Revenge Season 2

24 Season 6

24: Redemption

Haywire

Grey's Anatomy Season 9

Army Wives Season 7

Carjacked

Castle Season 5

Vampire Diaries Season 4

Once Upon A Time Season 2

The Perfect Age of Rock and Roll

Picture Day

Epic

Person of Interest Season 1

Premium Rush

World War Z

Identity Thief

Revolution Season 1

Suburgatory Season 1

Homeland Season 1

Sons of Anarchy Season 2

Sons of Anarchy Season 3

Sons of Anarchy Season 4

Sons of Anarchy Season 1

The Mentalist Season 5

The Croods

Turbo

2 Broke Girls Season 2

Arrow Season 1

Monster's University

Before Midnight

The Mortal Instruments: City of Bones

Girls Season 1

Man of Steel

Grimm Season 1

2014

Girls Season 2

Iron Man 3

Deadfall

The Mysterious Cities of Gold

It's A Disaster

Warm Bodies

Lovelace

CSI: Season 13

Warehouse 13 Season 2

Captain Phillips

Don Jon

Tiny Furniture

Grimm Season 2

Person of Interest Season 2

Awkward Season 3 Part 1

Despicable Me 2

Thieves (Korean)

Life's Too Short

Struck By Lightening

The Giant Mechanical Man

500 Days of Summer (Again)

Janie Jones

Pacific Rim

Game of Thrones Season 3

Mad Men Season 5

Homeland Season 2

The Lone Ranger

Catching Fire

The Walking Dead Season 2

The Walking Dead Season 3

The Walking Dead Season 1

Buffy The Vampire Season 4

Buffy The Vampire Season 3

Evening Harder: A Night With Kevin Smith

In Love and Honor

On The Road

Kill Your Darlings

Austenland

Saving Mr. Banks

Elementary Season 1

As Cool As I Am

Hackers (Again)

Kissing Jessica Stein (Again)

Rust and Bone

Jack the Giant Slayer

Thor: The Dark World

Despicable Me 2

How To Lose Your Lover

Some Girls

Imagine Me & You (Again)

Saving Face (Again)

Celeste and Jesse Forever

The Americans Season 1

Gravity

Crazy Kind of Love

Breathless

Generation Um

Smashed

Another Happy Day

Girls Season 1

Gone Baby Gone

Save the Date

The Odd Life of Timothy Green

John Adams

Out of the Furnace

Mythbusters Season 6, 8 and 9

This Is The End

Pompeii

We Are the Millers

Juno (Again)

Daredevil

The Secret Life of Walter Mitty

Warehouse 13 Season 1 and 2 (Again)

Trueblood Season 6

Nikita Season 4

The Hobbit: The Desolation of Smaug

The Wolf of Wallstreet

Covert Affairs Season 4

Good

A Dangerous Method

How To Train Your Dragon 2 (Theater)

Wonderlust

Warehouse 13 Season 5

Disengagement

Cosmopolis

The People Speak (Documentary)

The Road

Labor Day

Dallas Buyers Club

Winter's Tale

Trek Nation (Documentary)

Appaloosa (Again)

Choclat (Again)

Saved By The Bell Season 3 &4

Hidalgo (Again)

Happy Endings Seasons 1. 2 and 3

I, Frankenstein

The Lego Movie

Upside Down

Terra Nova

Guardians of the Galaxy (Theater)

Divergent

Transcendence

Once Upon A Time Season 3

The Book Thief

The Other Woman

Blended

Draft Day

Belle

Monuments Men

3 Days To Kill

Vikings Season 1

Grey's Anatomy Season 10

Homeland Season 3

Orange Is The New Black Season 1

Grimm Season 3

Captain America Winter Solider

The Fault in Our Stars

Movies Seen 2015

The Maze Runner

And So It Goes

House S4 (Again)

Mad Men S7

The Mentalist S3 and S4 (Again)

The Equalizer

Gone Girl

Reach Me

ER S5

Home Improvement S1 and S2

Maleficent (Again)

Dark City (Again)

The X-Files Season 1

The Two Faces of January

The Box Trolls

The Judge

Lucy

John Wick

Dracula Untold

MvGyver S1, S2 (Again)

Kissing Jessica Stein (Again)

True Romance (Again)

Red Shoe Diaries (Again)

The West Wing S1,S2, S3

Boston Legal S2

The Mentalist S1

Game of Thrones S4

Sons of Anarchy S7

Big Hero 6

The Book of Life

St. Vincent

Homesman

Birdman

House of Cards S1

Outlander S1 V1

Vikings S2

Black Sails S1

Mocking Jay Pt1

Wuthering Heights 1992 (Again)

Alexander and the Very Bad, Horrible Terrible No Good Day

The Penguins of Madagascar

Night at the Museum 3: Secret of the Tomb

The Walking Dead S1,S2 and S4 (Again)

Interstellar

Wild

Big Eyes

Romancing the Stone (Again)

The Quiet Man (1952)

Sleepy Hollow S1

The Hobbit: Battle of the 5 Armies

Wild Card

Cake

Taken 3

Ask Me Anything

The Giver

50 Shades of Grey

Upside Down (Again)

The Gambler

Still Alice

Inside Out (Theater)

Minions Movie (Theater)

Orange is the New Black S2

Orange is the New Black S3

Sponge Out of Water

Portlandia S1

Last Man Standing S1 & 2

The Carrie Diaries S1 & 2

The Outlander S1 V2

The Originals S1 &2

The Lego Movie (Again)

The Lorax (Again)

The Spear of Destiny (Again)

The Duff

Tomorrowland

The 100 S2

The Affair S1

Masters of Sex S3

Black Sails S2

August: Osage County (Stream)

Papertowns

Dune (2000) SyFy Mini-Series

Particle Fever (Stream)

The Man from UNCLE

Picture Day (Again)

Mission Impossible: Rogue Nation

Star Wars: The Force Awakens (Theater)

2016

American Sniper

Trainwreck

Clouds of Sila Marna

Amelie (Again)

Breaking Bad

Maze Runner: Scorch Trials

Ricki and The Flash

What If

Manhattan S1

The Martian

Mad Men Season 7 Part 2

The Affair Season 1 and 2

Masters of Sex Season 2

The Walking Dead Season 6

Goosebumps

A Walk in the Woods

Jem and the Holograms

The Intern

Love (Netflix Series)

Malcolm in the Middle (Again)

Barbie Spy Squad

Sicario

Ant Man

Appaloosa (Again)

Burnt

Game of Thrones S5

Manhattan S2

Mockingjay Pt 2

The Cosmos (Netflix)

Better Call Saul Season 1 and 2

Carol

Miss You Already

The Peanuts Movie

Zootopia (Theater)

Sisters

Girls Season 5 (HBO)

James Bond: Specter

Macbeth (2015)

Sleeping With Other People

He Named Me Malala

Pan

Batman V Superman

King Arthur (Again)

Turn Season 2

Alone Season 1 and 2

Game of Thrones Season 6 (HBO)

Macbeth (2016)

Point Break (2016)

Forsaken

Grandma

Deadpool

Orange is the New Black Season 4 (Netflix)

The Secret Life of Pets (Theater)

DVD Collection

2016

DVDs	Replacement or New	DVDs	Replacement or New
10 Things I Hate	New	HP: Deathly Hallows	New
13 Going on 30	New	Henry and June	New
(500) Days of Summer	New	The Incredibles	New
Agora	New	Indiana Jones Trilogy	Copy
Alice in Wonderland	New	Interview W/Vampire	Copy
Anastasia (Cartoon)	New	A Knight's Tale	Copy
Away We Go	New	Kama Sutra	Copy
Brave	New	King Arthur	Copy
Bourne Supremacy	New	Kissing Jessica Stein	Copy
Beauty and Beast	Copy	Labyrinth	Copy
Bad Santa	New	The Last Samurai	New
Catching Fire	New	The Last Unicorn	Copy
Cars	New	Legends of the Fall	Copy
Cars 2	New	Lemony Snicket's	New
Clerks	Copy	The Lion King	New
Chronicles: Dawn Treader	New	LOTR: Fellowship	New
Crouching Tiger, Hidden	Copy	LOTR: Two Towers	New
Celeste and Jessie	New	LOTR: Return King	New
Charlie Wilson's War	New	The Matrix	New
Cloudy With A Chance	New	Matrix Reloaded	New
Dangerous Beauty	Copy	Mona Lisa's Smile	New
Dark City	Copy	Minions	New
Dead Again	Copy	Mortal Instruments	New
Donnie Darko	New	Music and Lyrics	New
Dracula (Bram Stoker's)	Copy	My Life without Me	New

Drowning Mona	Copy	My So-Called Life	Copy
Dune SyFy Mini-Series	New	Nick and Nora	New
The English Patient	Copy	Princess Bride	Copy
Eastern Promises	New	Percy Jackson	New
Erin Brockovich	New	Red Shoe Diaries	Copy
Eternal Sunshine	New	Run Lola Run	Copy
Finding Nemo	New	Rush	Copy
The 5th Element	Copy	Secretary	New
Flesh and Bone	Copy	Serenity	New
Foxfire	Copy	Pinocchio	New
Furious Five	New	Pirates Caribbean	Copy
The Giant Mech Man	New	Shrek 2	New
Gargoyles S1 and S2	Copy	Shrek 3	New
Goonies	Copy	Sleeping Beauty	New
Grey's Anatomy S1	Copy	Snow White	New
HP: Sorcerer's Stone	New	Spiderman	Copy
HP: Chamber of Secrets	New	Stardust	New
HP: Prisoner of Azkaban	New	Star Wars II: Attack	New
		Star Wars III: Revenge	New
HP: Goblet of Fire	New	Sylvia	New
HP: Order of the Phoenix	New	True Romance	Copy
HP: Half Blood Prince	New		
When Harry Met Sally	Copy		
Willow	Copy		
Wings of Desire	Copy		
Wuthering Heights	Copy		
V For Vendetta	Copy		
X-Files: Fight	Copy		

TV SERIES

Alias S1-S5	Copy
Firefly	New
Fringe S2-S3	New
Game of Thrones S1-S5	New
Lost S1-S5	Copy
Party of Five S1	New
She-Ra S1-S2	Copy
The Simpsons S2 & S4	New

KID'S MOVIES

Barbie: Charm School	New
Barbie: Nutcracker	New
Barbie: Princess & Pauper	New
Barbie: Swan Lake	New
Barbie: Thumbelina	New
Johnny Test	New
Justice League	New
Leap Frog: Letter Factory	New
Leap Frog: Word Factory	New
Leap Frog: Let's Go To School	New
Leap Frog: Code Word Caper	New
Mona The Vampire	New
Phineas and Ferb	New
Sailor Moon	New
Sponge Bob: Love Patty	New
Teen Titans: Tokoyo	New

VHS Purchased

12 Monkeys

Age of Innocence

Braveheart

City of Angels

Closer

Conspiracy Theory

Contact

The Crow

Dark City

Dead Again

The Doors

Ever After

Flesh and Bone

Forget Paris

The Game

Good Will Hunting

Jade

Liar, Liar

Men In Black

Moonlight and Valentino

Nothing To Lose

Romeo + Juliet

Seven

Strange Days

Titanic

Out on A Limb

We Don't Live Here

U-Turn

The X-Files Fight The Future

Young Sherlock Holmes

Kid's Movie

Arthur Books

Arthur Music

Arthur Summer Fun

Babar

Bob The Builder

Caillou

Clifford the Big Red Dog (DVD)

Big Comfy Couch

Curious George (recorded)

Cyberchase (recorded)

Dragon Tales: Bravery (DVD)

Huffalump Movie

Magic School Bus: Baking

Magic School Bus: Music

Magic School Bus: Volcano

The Rugrats Movie

Rugrats Gone Wild

Peanuts: Christmas (DVD)

Peanuts: Great Pumpkin (DVD)

Peanuts: Thanksgiving (DVD)

Powerpuff Girls

Pooh's Great Adventure

Sagwa: The Chinese Siamese Cat

Tiger Movie

Thomas and Friends

Word Girl

Beauty and the Beast

Snow White

Sleeping Beauty

Little Mermaid

Little Mermaid 2

The Littlest Polar Bear

Cinderella

An American Tail

Land Before Time

Collections

Anne of Green Gables
Anne of Avonlea

Basic Instinct
Sliver
Showgirls

Brother's McMillan
She's The One

Dangerous Beauty
Wings of the Dove

Dracula
Lady in White
The Abyss

Dracula Dead and Loving It
Robin Hood Men In Tights
Spaceballs

Dreamer of Oz
Labyrinth
Last Unicorn

Few Good Men
The Mask
Speed

Flirting with Disaster
Feeling Minnesota
Love and a .45

Fried Green Tomatoes
The Neverending Story

House of the Spirits
Joy Club
Like Water For Chocolate

Johnny Neumonic

Once Were Warriors
Secrets and Lies

Pump Up The Volume
True Romance
Cuffs

Robin Hood: Prince of Thieves
Thunderheart

Ms Parker and Vicious Circle
Henry and June

Wuthering Heights
Kama Sutra: A Love Story
The English Patient

Rush
Basketball Diaries
Gia

Reality Bites
Clerks
Chasing Amy

Pulp Fiction
Four Rooms
From Dusk Until Dawn

Wings of Desire
Dreams
Belle De Jour

Red Shoe Diaries
Playing God
Foxfire

Necessary Parties
Born into Exile
Princess and The Marine

Saved By The Bell (Series)

Net
The Ghost

Ladyhawk
The Princess Bride

Prince of Tides
Beaches

Point Break
Dead Again

Raiders of the Lost Ark
Officer and a Gentleman
Mannequin

Revenge
Damage
Blue

Shawshank Redemption
Thelma and Louise

When Harry Met Sally
Sleepless in Seattle
You've Got Mail

The Way We Were
Love Story
Romeo and Juliet

Wild Orchid
Wild Orchid: 2 Shades of Blue
9 ½ Weeks

Willow
The Last Crusade

My So-Called Life (Series)

Alias (Series)

Lost (Series)

The X-Files (Series)

Gargoyles (Series)

Relativity (Series)

Shadetree Mechanic (Jason Series)

Music Videos

Music Videos

The Life Home Video Skits

Bull in A China Shop
Making It (School Plays)

Graduation from UNCG

Gilkison Family Reunion 1990

Mariah Carey First Vision
Mariah Carey Compilation/Specials

TV Shows That I Watched Frequently

Nick At Nite (50s and 60s Reruns)

The Donna Reed Show

Patty Duke

Hazel

I Love Lucy

Dennis the Menace

Leave It to Beaver

Lassie

My Three Sons

Mary Tyler Moore Show

Rhoda

Bewitched

I Dream of Jeanne

Gidget

The Flying Nun

Flipper

The Monkees

Green Acres

Addams Family

The Munsters

Lost in Space

Star Trek

Twilight Zone

The Outer Limits

70s Shows (Reruns)

Buck Rogers

Happy Days

Laverne and Shirley

The Brady Bunch

M*A*S*H

Gilligan's Island

The Beverly Hillbillies

The Walton's

Little House on the Prairie

Carol Burnette Show

The Partridge Family

Eight Is Enough

The Muppet Show

The 6 Million Dollar Man

Spiderman

The Incredible Hulk

Wonder Woman

Alice

CHiPs

Charlie's Angles

All In The Family

Sandford and Sons

Maude

Highway To Heaven

Heaven Help Us

Mama's Family

Three's Company

Different Strokes

Facts of Life

Punky Bruster

Small Wonder

ER (Comedy)

Gimme a Break

Designing Women

Kate and Allie

Family Ties

Growing Pains

Just the 10 of Us

Head of the Class

My Two Dads

227

Amen

MacGyver

Night Court

Tailspin

Gummy Bears

The Smurf

The Snorkles

Shirt Tales

Alvin and Chipmunks

Strawberry Shortcake

Rainbow Brite

Moonlighting

Dallas

Falcon Crest

The Dukes of Hazard

Magnum PI

Murder She Wrote

Charles in Charge

Double Trouble

Quantum Leap

Star Trek The Next Gen

Doogie Howser MD

The Wonder Years

David the Gnome

Spartakus Land Beneath Sea

The Mysterious Cities Gold

He-Man

She-ra

Inspector Gadget

Dangerous Mouse

Double Dare

You Can't Do That On TV

Belle and Sebastian

Jem and The Holograms

The Cosby Show

It's A Different World

Crossbow

Cover Up

Partners in Crime

Star Man

Rosanne

Golden Girls

Empty Nest

Murphy Brown

Who's The Boss

Wings

Dr. Quinn Medicine Woman

Sisters

Reasonable Doubt

Beverly Hills 90210

ER

Ellen (Comedy)

The Simpsons

Fresh Prince of Bel Air

Family Matters

Blossom

Home Improvement

Friends

Caroline in the City

Suddenly Susan

The Naked Truth

Single Guy

Grace Under Fire

Drew Carey

Cybil

Something So Right

Step By Step

Melrose Place

Grace Under Fire

Party of Five

Charmed

Judging Amy

Felicity

Dawson's Creek

Hercules

Xenia

Buffy The Vampire Slayer

The X-Files

Mad About You

Saved By The Bell

Dharma and Greg

Futurama

Bevis and Butthead

Daria

King of the Hill

Sabrina The Teenage Witch

Seinfeld

Picket Fences

Ally McBeal

Boston Public

My So-Called Life

Relativity

Northern Exposure

Dave's World

Veronica's Closet

Becker

Jeff Foxworthy Show

Reba

2000s

Dark Angel

CSI

Alias

Lost

Fringe

Sex in the City

Grey's Anatomy

Bones

House

CSI NY

Prison Break

The Mentalist

Mythbusters

Malcolm in the Middle

How I Met Your Mother

Grounded For Life

Scrubs

Heroes

That 70s Show

Firefly

King of Queens

My Name is Earl

What I Like About You

Weeds

The L-Word

Dead Like Me

Pushing Daisies

Castle

Trueblood

Covert Affairs

2010s

Grimm

Elementary

Arrow

The Flash

Two Broke Girls

iZombie

Blacklist

Once Upon A Time

The Walking Dead

Mad Men

Breaking Bad

Better Call Saul

Person of Interest

Revolution

Raising Hope

Last Man Standing

Game of Thrones

The Affair

Masters of Sex

Outlander

Homeland

Black Sails

Vikings

Sons of Anarchy

The Americans

Into The Badlands

Bastard Executioner

The Middle

The Goldbergs

Mike and Molly

www.ingramcontent.com/pod-product-compliance
Lightning Source LLC
Chambersburg PA
CBHW081405280526
45788CB00009B/2991